GW00691800

1791

THE OBSERVER

More Sayings of the Week

Selected and compiled by
Colin Cross

David & Charles
Newton Abbot   London   North Pomfret (Vt)

British Library Cataloguing in Publication Data

More sayings of the week.
  1. Quotations, English
  I. Cross, Colin
  828'.9'140208   PN6081

  ISBN 0–7153–8448–1

Typeset by ABM Typographics Ltd, Hull
and printed in Great Britain
by Butler & Tanner Limited, Frome and London
for David & Charles (Publishers) Limited
Brunel House   Newton Abbot   Devon

Published in the United States of America
by David & Charles Inc
North Pomfret   Vermont 05053   USA

Introduction

'Sayings of the Week' have run in *The Observer* since 1908, with gaps, and are reckoned to be memorable, at least at the end of the week in question. While obviously they have a strongly British bias, we do try to make them international, and the present collection comes from many countries.

One test is that they must be 'of the week' and so, if we do not catch them fresh, they are lost for our purposes. It could seem that the most notable omission in the present collection, in terms of British domestic politics, is Mr Norman Tebbit's supposed advice to the unemployed to 'get on your bike'. But in fact Mr Tebbit did not say quite that. He referred only to his unemployed father in the 1930s getting on his bike in search of work, which was not really a Saying, and the words passed into political currency in an adapted form. For our purposes there are plenty of statements that can be used without adaptation, as with Mr Andropov on unilateral nuclear disarmament, Pope John Paul II on a man committing adultery with his wife, and Ayatollah Khomeini on cutting off people's hands.

We pick up in 1979 from where the last book collection *Sayings of the Seventies* finished and take them up to the end of 1982. It has been a vivid period with Mrs Margaret Thatcher, Pope John Paul II, Ayatollah Khomeini, Mr Menachem Begin and various members of the British Royal Family all batting with vigour.

The dates given are those of the Sunday on which the quotations appeared in *The Observer*. Titles and styles are those in force when the words were spoken, and are kept to the minimum needed for identification.

Colin Cross

Actors and Acting

Kissing is harder than taking off your clothes.

Sylvia Kristel, 30.3.1980

His comedy was based on truth, which is the essence of all great comedy.

Ian Carmichael, on Peter Sellers, 27.7.1980

We actors are the damned of the earth.

Sophia Loren, 31.8.1980

There is no particular reason why the honestly held political views of actors and actresses should carry any more or less weight than those of plumbers.

Peter Plouviez, Equity, 12.10.1980

People laugh only when they feel secure.

Penelope Keith, 18.1.1981

Show business is like life. You don't know how long it's going to last so you may as well enjoy it while you can.

Frankie Howerd, 8.3.1981

It's a miracle to have a straight play on Broadway for more than two nights, especially when it's not British.

Swoosie Kurtz, 2.8.1981

I just never had the luck to play bitches. Those are the only parts that ever register really.

Claudette Colbert, 13.9.1981

The director is the most overrated artist in the world.

Orson Welles, 7.3.1982

It's the only time I would commit murder. I would actually shoot somebody at that time, just shoot 'em down and stomp on them. Bastards!

Frank Capra, on seeing cut versions of his films on television, 2.5.1982

Ambitions

I would like to go to Scotland. People say it is so beautiful and so peaceful.

Prime Minister Maria de Lourdes Pintasilgo of Portgugal,
2.9.1979

I have seen so many people destroyed by personal ambition.

Tony Benn, 25.9.1979

Of course, I wouldn't just like to be involved in the bits and bobs of politics. I would like to be Prime Minister.

Kevin Keegan, 18.11.1979

All I ever wanted was a nice little house in North Oxford and a don for a husband.

Lady Wilson, 24.2.1980

They may, in the fullness of time, even canonise me and make me a saint.

Derek (Red Robbo) Robinson, 24.2.1980

In my opinion, all motorcycles should be banned.

Dr Herbert Pilling, South Yorkshire coroner, 2.11.1980

What the system pays doctors, politicians and senior managerial staff should also be paid to miners.

Arthur Scargill, 11.7.1982

Personally I hope never to see any ice ever again.

Sir Ranulph Fiennes, 8.8.1982

Animals

I don't think dogs have much fun nowadays without things like rats to chase.

Barbara Woodhouse, 21.9.1980

If your home burns down, rescue the dogs. At least they'll be faithful to you.

Lee Marvin, 28.9.1980

Some of my best leading men have been dogs and horses.

Elizabeth Taylor, 22.2.1981

People come up to me, shake my hand, shout 'Walkies' and scream with laughter.

Barbara Woodhouse in Los Angeles, 6.9.1981

We tell our men never to show fear of growling dogs.

Postmaster Charles Owen of Aylesbury, 29.8.1982

Aphorisms

To be five or ten minutes early is a sign of efficiency. To be half an hour early is wasting time.

C. Northcote Parkinson, 18.11.1979

Man is more than a rational being; but the adoration of the irrational can justify horrible crimes.

Ralf Dahrendorf, 18.11.1979

Governments never learn. Only people learn.

Milton Friedman, 30.3.1980

If you don't like black people, don't come to Africa.

Sir Roy Welensky, 20.4.1980

The cliché 'charity begins at home' has done more damage than any other in the English tongue.

Bishop Trevor Huddleston, 14.9.1980

Where human beings are directly affected, small steps are infinitely more important than big words.

Willy Brandt, 5.10.1980

There is a lot to be said in schools and in communities generally for seeing that nobody is below the rank of lance-corporal.

Rhodes Boyson, 23.11.1980

You can tell a lot about a fellow's character by the way he eats jelly beans.

President Reagan, 25.1.1981

It's no good telling a man: 'Look, if you behave well, in 35 generations' time your son will have a slightly larger brain than you.'

Benny Green, 15.2.1981

When you have protruding teeth like mine, you have to keep smiling.

Sir Peter Parker, 22.2.1981

A man who is old enough to die for his country is old enough to be able to decide whom to sleep with.

Council for Gay Teenagers, 12.4.1981

When one is President of the Republic, one cannot say 'I'll wait and see.'

Giscard d'Estaing, 10.5.1981

There were two revolutions in the early twentieth century. One was the revolution in morals and the other was the revolution in money.

William Rees-Mogg, 14.6.1981

Wars make for better reading than peace does.

A J P Taylor, 5.7.1981

Having seen what my injuries were, I knew it was not necessary to die.

Lt-Gen Sir Steuart Pringle, blown up by a car bomb, 25.10.1981

There is more truth in the bedroom than in the office or boardroom.

François Truffaut, 1.11.1981

Moderation is a virtue only in those who are thought to have an alternative.

Henry Kissinger, 24.1.1982

7

One change of country is enough for a lifetime.

George Mikes, 21.2.1982

When you go in search of honey, you must expect to be stung by bees.

President Kaunda, 9.5.1982

There are few things more painful than to recognise one's own faults in others.

John Wells, 23.5.1982

A certain amount of judicious snobbery is quite a good thing, besides being amusing.

A L Rowse, 20.6.1982

Men play the game; women know the score.

Roger Woddis, 11.7.1982

I can always judge people by the way they ring my doorbell.

Cynthia Payne, the former madam at Streatham,
17.10.1982

Aristocrats

I'm not a social person but I could fall for a duke — they are a great aphrodisiac.

Tina Brown, Editor, The Tatler. 7.10.1979

It doesn't necessarily follow that noblemen behave in a particularly noble manner towards their wives.

Lady Lucan, 25.10.1979

Whether it's Peugeots or perfume, don't buy it from the French.

Duke of Buccleuch, 4.11.1979

I will exterminate the filthy little worm.

Marchioness of Reading, on Dai Llewellyn, 16.3.1980

Everyone has ancestors.

Debrett *advertisement, 18.5.1980*

I'm pretty fed up with being known as Nancy Mitford's brother-in-law.

Duke of Devonshire, 1.6.1980

I don't like being recognised in the street.

Lord Carrington, 22.6.1980

He's in favour of letting people out of jail, and I'm more in favour of keeping them there.

Lord Langford on Lord Longford, 29.6.1980

One is only equal when dead.

Viscount Masserene and Ferrard, 3.5.1981

Property is not just bricks and mortar.

Duke of Westminster, 10.5.1981

If you don't know how many rooms you have got, you have got too many.

Countess Spencer, 6.12.1981

I don't know exactly how many rooms there are. My best count is somewhere between 130 and 140.

George Howard, on Castle Howard, 14.2.1982

Arts and Architecture

Sometimes one has thought of the Arts Council as culture subsidising its own overthrow.

Roy Fuller, 9.12.1979

I have always thought my pictures were too expensive.

David Hockney, 27.7.1980

To close Southend Pier would be like cutting off a limb.

Sir John Betjeman, 3.8.1980

Can anyone draw up a list of five buildings in London worth a detour to see, which have been put up since the war?

Jo Grimond, 31.5.1981

Britain, the British

People in England are so bloody nosey.

Elton John, 11.11.1979

In spite of a few historical accidents — Joan of Arc, Fashoda, Waterloo — we have always admired our British friends' cool-headedness, fair play and skill at understatement.

France-Soir, 6.4.1980

The English are probably the most tolerant, least religious people on earth.

Rabbi David Goldberg, 20.4.1980

Though the English pride themselves on their sense of humour, they distrust humorous men.

Lord Annan, 2.11.1980

I believe that the result of the Battle of Hastings dealt a blow to brevity from which our language has never recovered.

Lord Kings Norton, 1.2.1981

There's never been a holiday like this. For £30 you can join the ranks of 40 paying prisoners of war at a chillingly realistic Colditz-style concentration camp.

Great British Alternative Holiday Catalogue, 12.4.1981

The sun never set on the British Empire because God doesn't trust the Brits in the dark.

IRA placard in New York, 21.6.1981

How many people in Britain recognise that we export as a percentage of our national production twice as much as the Japanese?

Sir Raymond Pennock, CBI, 28.6.1981

The English language is like a juggernaut truck that goes on regardless.

Robert Burchfield, Oxford English Dictionary, 25.10.1981

One gets the impression from the popular Press that rape has become the British national pastime.

Lord Wigoder, 24.1.1982

It was in 1066 that William the Conqueror occupied Britain, stole our land and gained control by granting it to his Norman friends, thus creating the feudal system we have not yet fully escaped.

Tony Benn, 4.4.1982

The pervasive and popular stereotype of the drunken Scot is a myth.

Glasgow University Sociology Department, 29.8.1982

Candour

I don't like baths. I don't enjoy them in the slightest and if I could, I'd prefer to go around dirty.

J B Priestley, 16.9.1979

One man wrote and said he was going to kill me — but he gave his name and address.

Tony Benn, 30.9.1979

Chaplin was a most terrible phoney.

Laurence Olivier, 2.12.1979

I haven't the faintest idea what would be a good investment in antiques today. If I had, I'd be going round the world in my own yacht.

Arthur Negus, 3.8.1980

On three or four occasions I have come very close to saying: 'Sod it.'

Angela Rippon, 12.10.1980

The underarm delivery was an act of cowardice. It was appropriate that the Australian team was wearing yellow.

Prime Minister Robert Muldoon of New Zealand, 8.2.1981

The President doesn't want any yes men and women around him. When he says no, we all say no.

Elizabeth Hanford Dole, White House aide, 24.5.1981

We all know foreigners are difficult to deal with. Having shown Mrs Reagan round St Paul's, I know this for a fact.

Dean of St Paul's, 2.8.1981

Photographers are the most loathesome inconvenience. They're merciless. They're the pits.

Paul Newman, 25.10.1981

When it came to writing about wine, I did what almost everybody does — faked it.

Art Buchwald, 30.5.1982

All cars being driven today are obsolete in terms of safety.

Ben Kelly, US Insurance Institute, 26.9.1982

China

Peace cannot be got by begging. War cannot be averted by yielding.

Chairman Hua Guofeng, 4.11.1979

Art for art's sake is the philosophy of the well-fed.

Cao Yu, Playwright, 13.4.1980

China will emerge as a tremendous economic and military power in the 21st century.

Japanese Institute of Foreign Affairs, 31.8.1980

After you have been to the washroom, properly secure your belt and button up your pants before coming out.

Workers' Daily, *Peking,* 22.3.1981

Comrades at the lower level must respect and obey the leadership of comrades at a higher level.

Chairman Hua Guofeng, 5.7.1981

Christians

Alcoholism among priests and religious orders is increasing and is a problem of world dimensions.

Fr Joseph McNamara, Superior-General, Servants of the Holy Paraclete, 9.12.1979

Those countries with legalised abortion are the poorest countries in the world.

Mother Teresa, 16.12.1979

I find it scandalous that a church which is based on Jesus Christ, and which recently has started to defend human rights, stages Inquisition cases in the twentieth century.

Hans Küng, 23.12.1979

I believe I have demonic forces opposed to me wherever I preach.

Billy Graham, 3.2.1980

Jesus said love one another. He didn't say love the whole world.

Mother Teresa, 2.3.1980

The task of the Church now is to cope with people who want to do something more serious than change the flowers every week.

Archbishop of Canterbury, 23.3.1980

I believe that God created man. I object to teachers saying that we came from monkeys.

Ian Paisley, 27.4.1980

Lambeth Palace is rather difficult to make into a home.

Mrs Rosalind Runcie, 8.6.1980

France, eldest daughter of the Church, are you faithful to the promises of your baptism?

Pope John Paul II, 8.6.1980

Only a socially just society has the right to exist.

Pope John Paul, II, 6.7.1980

The blood of the martyrs cries out against this visit.

Ian Paisley, on the Pope's visit to Britain, 7.9.1980

There is a serious need in the Christian churches to affirm strongly to today's world our common belief in the existence of the Evil One.

Cardinal Suenens, 21.9.1980

Such persons are often good, conscientious and faithful sons and daughters of the Church.

Cardinal Hume, on Roman Catholics who use contraceptives, 5.10.1980

Adultery in your heart is committed not only when you look with excessive sexual desire at a woman who is not your wife, but also if you look in the same manner at your wife.

Pope John Paul II, 5.10.1980

The General Synod has made a bit of a mess of the Lord's Prayer.

Bishop of Durham, 12.4.1981

Christianity and trade unionism are practically synonymous — good trade unionism.

Terry Duffy, 19.4.1981

As a Roman Catholic I thank God for the heretics. Heresy is only another word for freedom of thought.

Graham Greene, 19.4.1981

Christ never promised a 'no-risk' pilgrimage.

Archbishop of Canterbury, 17.5.1981

We shall not perish as a people even if we get our money supply wrong — but if we get our human relationships wrong, we shall destroy ourselves.

Archbishop of Canterbury, 19.7.1981

There is no doubt that in British political terms the Pope is a wet.

Norman St John-Stevas, 20.9.1981

I cannot see how God can possibly sort us out when we get to the gates of heaven or hell.

Barbara Woodhouse, 18.10.1981

Creation of the world out of nothing is the ultimate religious statement, because God is the only actor.

US Federal Judge William Overton, at Little Rock, 10.1.1982

Thanks be to Allah.

Pope John Paul II, in Nigeria, 21.2.1982

It has always struck me as rather strange that in a supposedly Christian country an agnostic was considered preferable to a Roman Catholic for the top job in the BBC.

Sir Hugh Greene, 9.5.1982

Christianity is the most materialistic of the world's religions.

Donald Soper, 13.6.1982

There is, mercifully, still something so magical about Sunday morning, a feeling that not all the secularising of the day can destroy.

Mary Whitehouse, 15.8.1982

Hearts who seek quarrels understand nothing of God — and just as little of human needs.

Archbishop Glemp, 5.9.1982

Civil Servants and Diplomats

The Civil Service always hopes it is influencing Ministers towards the common ground.

Sir Anthony Part, former Permanent Secretary, Department of Industry, 7.12.1980

As a trained diplomat, it was an aberration on my part.

Sir Geoffrey Harrison on his affair with a Soviet chambermaid, 1.3.1981

Britain has invented a new missile. It's called the civil
servant — it doesn't work and it can't be fired.

General Sir Walter Walker, 15.3.1981

At the Embassy in Paris only 52 per cent of the
Diplomatic Service staff have the ability to use French
adequately or better.

Commons Select Committee on the Foreign Office,
26.7.1981

Many junior civil servants are taking home less than £45
a week, and you cannot expect loyalty for that sort of
money.

Union official at the Welsh Office, 10.9.1981

Conservatives

Were the Tories to elect a 'national executive' and to do
so annually at Brighton or Blackpool, the first three
names would read: 'Michael Heseltine, Rhodes Boyson
and Reggie Prentice.'

Julian Critchley, MP, 14.10.1979

I have nothing against Hampstead. I used to live there
myself in the days when I was an intellectual. I gave that
up when I became Leader of the House.

Norman St John-Stevas, 18.5.1980

I really don't know what a wet is.

William Whitelaw, 23.1.1980

The loss of one's job is a misfortune which should be
borne with dignity and reticence.

Norman St John-Stevas, 11.1.1981

I did not go into politics to be a kamikaze pilot.

John Biffen, 1.3.1981

If you take yourself too seriously in politics, you've had
it.

Lord Carrington, 24.5.1981

It does no harm to throw the occasional man overboard, but it does not do much good if you are steering full ahead for the rocks.

Sir Ian Gilmour, 20.9.1981

You see, I'm a Conservative and I don't think politics are frightfully important.

John Nott, 19.9.1982

Definitions

Terrorism is armed propaganda.

Maj-Gen Sir Frank Kitson, Commandant, Army Staff College, 13.1.1980

A man's nation is the nation for which he will fight.

Enoch Powell, 22.2.1981

Italy is a poor country full of rich people.

Richard Gardner, former US Ambassador in Rome, 16.8.1981

Positivity is news. Negativity is not news.

Justin Nyoka, Zimbabwe Director of Information, 25.10.1981

The word 'meaningful' when used today is nearly always meaningless.

Paul Johnson, 25.7.1982

Dogma

Most people's opinions are of no value at all.

A L Rowse, 26.8.1979

Life *is* unfair.

Milton Friedman, 13.4.1980

Men and women will retain their sex in heaven.

Pope John Paul II, 6.12.1981

You can't be a feminist and a capitalist.

Ruth Wallsgrove, Spare Rib, 25.7.1982

Economy

We are drinking in the Last Chance Saloon.

Sir John Methven, Director General, CBI, 11.11.1979

The industrialised countries can pay whatever we ask.

Libyan Petroleum Minister Izzedin Mabrouk, 23.12.1979

The average family spends 15 per cent of its income on beer, baccy, bingo and Benidorm and only 2 to 3 per cent on electricity.

Alex Young, North-East Electricity Board, 20.1.1980

You must give the nationalised industries away.

Milton Friedman, 2.3.1980

Punk monetarism is a monetary philosophy based on half-baked understanding of half-baked dogmas.

Denis Healey, 30.3.1980

If a film costs five million dollars and looks as if it cost 10 million, that's good, but if it looks as if it cost only four million, that's wrong.

Clint Eastwood, 21.9.1980

There is a difference between a bracing climate and freezing to death.

Sir Maurice Hodgson, Chairman of ICI, 26.10.1980

God wants us to be rich and comfortable.

Walter Hoving, Chairman of Tiffany's, 30.11.1980

I don't know that I'm in the 20th century — I may be in the 18th or 21st.

Ian Macgregor, Chairman of British Steel, 18.1.1981

Petrol is still cheaper than milk.

Nicholas Fairbairn MP, 3.5.1981

Money is as much a reality as the Blessed Trinity.

Monsignor Ralph Brown, co-ordinator of the Papal visit to Britain, 28.6.1981

We are at the end of the recession.

Sir Geoffrey Howe, 2.8.1981

We are actually selling spaghetti to Italy, bulbs to Holland and brussels sprouts to Brussels.

Peter Walker, 18.10.1981

Conflict over wages is inescapable in industry.

Arthur Scargill, 10.1.1982

Keeping the books has a wonderfully salutory effect on a man.

Enoch Powell, 14.2.1982

Europe

Europe is the real zone of peace, the only one in the world.

Egon Bahr, West German Social Democratic Party, 6.1.1980

European Community institutions have produced European beets, butter, cheese, wine, veal and even pigs. But they have not produced Europeans.

Louise Weiss, MEP, 27.1.1980

We shall be bloody to them. They will be bloody back. And then we shall just be even more bloody.

British Cabinet Minister on the EEC, quoted in The Guardian, 9.3.1980

The last time Britain went into Europe with any degree of success was on 6 June 1944.

Daily Express, 23.3.1980

Shut up or get out.

Jacques Chirac on Britain and the EEC, 23.3.1980

The EEC simply is not functioning well enough.

Willy Brandt, 12.7.1981

If Europe has no better reason for its own defence than to please an American administration, then we are all in trouble.

Henry Kissinger, 2.8.1981

Falklands

It was very similar to my departure from Vietnam.

Governor Rex Hunt, 11.4.1982

The conflict over the Falklands is a moment dislodged from its natural home in the late nineteenth century.

Lance Morrow, 18.4.1982

This is the run-up to the big match which, in my view, should be a walkover.

Rear Admiral Sandy Woodward, Task Force commander, 2.5.1982

Unless people say 'let's stop' it will be a long and bloody conflict.

Rear Admiral Sandy Woodward, Task Force commander, 2.5.1982

From Michael Foot's statements, one would draw the conclusion that Labour is in favour of warmongering, provided there is no war.

Labour Herald, 2.5.1982

The widow of Portsmouth is no different from the widow of Buenos Aires.

Richard Francis, Managing Director, BBC radio, 16.5.1982

To have turned the other cheek would have meant that we should have become accomplices in making the world an even less stable place.

Archbishop of Canterbury, 30.5.1982

The Church in our country wants to co-operate in the building of a new Argentina, nourished with generous blood of our youth and the quiet tears of our mothers.

> *Independence Day sermon in Buenos Aires cathedral,*
> *30.5.1982*

War should belong to the tragic past, to history.

> *Pope John Paul II, 6.6.1982*

I feel very proud, even though they didn't elect me, to be President of the Argentines.

> *General Galtieri, 6.6.1982*

I should have thought it's purpose-built as a tourist attraction.

> *Enoch Powell, on the Falklands, 6.6.1982*

The working class boys were sent in to fight so that the bankers didn't have a default.

> *Tony Benn, 20.6.1982*

Until my dying day I shall never get out of my head the belief that this was an unnecessary war.

> *James Callaghan, 11.7.1982*

Fashion

There is always a seasonal demand for French knickers just before Christmas.

> *Marks & Spencer spokesman, 16.3.1980*

I know of only one civil servant in Whitehall who still comes to work in a bowler hat.

> *Sir Ian Bancroft, Head of the Civil Service, 14.12.1980*

Never trust a man whose tie is habitually an inch below his collar.

> *Letter in* The Times. 5.7.1981

Expensive clothes are a waste of money.

> *Meryl Streep, 18.10.1981*

Food and Drink

I'm very fond of my pigs; but I don't find it difficult to eat them.

Archbishop of Canterbury, 30.3.1980

The French drink to get loosened up for an event, to celebrate an event, and even to recover from an event.

Genevieve Guerin, French Commission on Alcoholism,
3.8.1980

I love entertaining. I have someone else to do the cooking, that's why.

Joan Plowright, 23.11.1980

The right diet directs sexual energy into the parts that matter.

Barbara Cartland, 11.1.1981

I mostly drink rather cheap wine and I like very simple food — cottage pie or fish cakes.

Roy Jenkins, 22.2.1981

There is no good reason why an English meal cooked by a Chinese and served by an Italian should be given a French name.

Clement Freud, 3.5.1981

I had my first whiskey sour when I was 14, and thought 'God, I've found a friend.' It was only a few years ago, when I thought our friendship was getting too steady, that I gave it up.

Elaine Stritch, 23.8.1981

What is traditional British cooking? We only have a few museum-pieces, such as Lancashire hot pot.

Egon Ronay, 14.2.1982

It is all right to call it a Swiss roll in the United Kingdom and possibly Canada, but not anywhere else.

Swiss Embassy spokesman on British-made Swiss rolls
sold in the Middle East, 4.4.1982

India

In the social set-up of modern India, cricket is the one sure way to gain acceptance.

Mihir Bose, 10.1.1982

I would not say that the poor are poorer, except that they are more conscious of it.

Indira Gandhi, 1.8.1982

Ireland

Paisley has been, and remains, a greater threat to the Union than the Foreign Office and the Provisional IRA rolled into one.

Enoch Powell, 11.1.1981

Wouldn't it be nice for the British Government to have me eliminated?

Ian Paisley, 22.11.1981

The informality of Irish life is one of the best things we have. But it can degenerate into an unselective acceptance of buffoonery and sleveenism.

Irish Times, 10.10.1982

We are looking for a wealth tax that will bring in sufficient revenue to justify having a wealth tax.

Dick Spring, leader of the Irish Labour Party, 5.12.1982

Israel

You cannot get Arab opinion by sitting and talking to Jews.

Moshe Dayan, 2.9.1979

The world does not understand the Palestinian problem.

Mayor Fahd Kawasmeh of Hebron, 18.5.1980

Someone must rule Jerusalem. Among all the rulers, we are the best.

Mayor Teddy Kollek of Jerusalem, 2.11.1980

To say that peace is some kind of favour to Israel is absolute nonsense; the Arabs need peace just as badly as we do.

Shimon Peres, 22.2.1981

If both sides don't want war, how can war break out?

Menachem Begin, 3.5.1981

Israel has nothing to apologise for.

Menachem Begin, 14.6.1981

Begin is a danger to democracy.

Shimon Peres, 21.6.1981

We will never take any military action that is not necessary.

Yitzhak Shamir, 20.12.1981

I will not apologise to Mr Schmidt.

Menachem Begin, 28.2.1982

When there is thunder and it rains, the snakes come out from under the rocks.

Mayor Elias Freij of Bethlehem, 20.6.1982

Of course we've got a guilty conscience, and rightly so. That's what makes us different.

Israeli Defence Ministry spokesman, 20.6.1982

My generation, dear Ron, swore on the Altar of God that whoever proclaims the intent to destroy the Jewish State or the Jewish people, or both, seals his fate.

Menachem Begin in a letter to President Reagan, 8.8.1982

We have expected the Arabs, but no one came. We have expected our friends in the world, but no one came

PLO newspaper in Beirut, 15.8.1982

No one will preach to us ethics and respect for human life, values in which we have educated, and will continue to educate, generations of Jewish fighters.

Menachem Begin, 26.9.1982

Jews

We have never given instructions to Jewish voters and will never do so. In any case they would be disobeyed.

Chief Rabbi Jacob Kaplan of Paris, 1.6.1980

There is always a danger in Judaism of seeing history as a sort of poker game played between Jews and God, in which the presence of others is noted but not given much importance.

Rabbi Lionel Blue, 29.8.1982

Khomeini

Male chauvinist is a simple, idiotic way of describing him.

Kate Millet on Ayatollah Khomeini, 18.3.1979

Even if this traitor Shah hides himself in a corner of the White House, we will get him out and kill him.

Ayatollah Khomeini, 1.7.1979

I hope we are not going the way of Iran where policemen, just because they wear blue uniform, are summarily rounded up and executed.

Mayor Frank Rizzo of Philadelphia, 19.8.79

The Kurds who are being executed do not belong to the Kurdish people.

Ayatollah Khomeini, 14.10.79

All over Washington people are now speed-reading the Koran.

Henry Fairlie, 9.12.1979

The people of Iran want to be martyrs.

Ayatollah Khomeini, 23.12.1979

I believe that the Ayatollah Khomeini is an Islamic heretic.

Dr Robert Runcie, Archbishop-designate of Canterbury,
30.12.1979

We are ready to accept the martyrdom of our children in England but we will not give in to blackmail.

President Bani-Sadr of Iran, on the embassy siege, 4.5.1980

A learned man who is not cleansed is more dangerous than an ignorant man.

Ayatollah Khomeini, 6.7.1980

Throwing stones certainly teaches people a lesson.

Ayatollah Khalkhali, 13.7.1980

The agreement with Iran for the return of the hostages has the same moral standing as an agreement with a kidnapper, that is to say none at all.

Wall Street Journal, 25.1.1981

I'll cut everybody's hands off.

Ayatollah Khomeini, 14.6.1981

France is a centre of hell.

President Rajai of Iran, 23.8.1981

I am like a child who watched as his father became an alcoholic before his very eyes.

Ex-President Bani-Sadr of Iran, on Ayatollah Khomeini, 6.9.1981

Today, without a doubt, we don't have the best situation in our judicial system.

President Ali Khameini of Iran, 21.2.1982

Labour Party

I'm no ghost.

James Callaghan, 8.6.1980

When a new set of Labour Ministers enter Number 10, as I trust they soon will, are they all to keep diaries? It will add a new terror to political life.

Michael Foot, 28.9.1980

The Labour Party is never to be taken more seriously
than when it looks as if it is destroying itself.

Enoch Powell, 12.10.1980

People can say what they want in the Labour Party.

Michael Foot, 25.1.1981

Every serious politician should keep a diary.

Barbara Castle, 8.3.1981

Elections are so healing.

Tony Benn, 5.4.1981

Go home and guard your backs.

Eric Ogden, MP, to fellow Labour MPs, 14.6.1981

I fear that within ten years there will be a coup and that
gays, trade union activists and left-wing politicians will
be led off to the gas chambers.

Ken Livingstone, 23.8.1981

There is too much fratricide, too little fraternity.

John Silkin, 13.9.1981

If people cannot resolve their crisis of housing, of jobs
and pensions through Parliament, they simply take to
the streets.

Tony Benn, 20.9.1981

I would like to tell you the secrets of what happened in
the last Labour Cabinet — but I haven't been in as many
Labour Cabinets as Tony has.

Michael Foot, 4.10.1981

There is no transport system on this planet that breaks
even, let alone makes a profit.

Ken Livingstone, 20.12.1981

There are certainly strange happenings within Loch Ness.

*David Wiseman, Labour candidate at the Glasgow Hillhead
by-election*, 17.1.1982

I am not a pacifist.

Michael Foot, 11.4.1982

All MPs must live on the average pay of a skilled worker,
plus genuine expenses vetted by the party.

Militant, 12.9.1982

Hazlitt's better than Hattersley.

Michael Foot, 26.9.1982

Law and Order

I utterly deplore and condemn any suggestion of killing
the Pope.

Ian Paisley, 10.9.1979

There's no certainty in the law.

Lord Denning, 30.9.1979

I don't think the police are always right.

Sir Thomas Hetherington, Director of Public Prosecutions,
4.11.1979

Professor Blunt has no statement to make. He feels
bound by the Official Secrets Act.

Statement on his behalf, 18.11.1979

I would not call it spying, what I did. It was just letting
Burgess see some notes I had made.

John Cairncross, 30.12.1979

If a woman is attacked, her best weapon is her lungs.

Chief Inspector Keith Killbride, West Yorkshire, 24.2.1980

Lies are told in criminal cases. Lies are told in civil
cases. Lies are told all the time.

Sir Michael Havers, Attorney General, 23.3.1980

Parliament itself would not exist in its present form had
people not defied the law.

Arthur Scargill, 6.4.1980

Truncheons are flimsy things.

Inspector Douglas Hopkins, Special Control Group,
11.5.1980

Sometimes even lawyers need lawyers.

Billy Carter, 27.7.1980

Juries are not good at distinguishing between good and bad policemen.

Lord Devlin, 27.7.1980

I think a policeman is a more imposing figure, and more likely to gain the respect of the yobbo, if he is six feet tall.

President Mike Bricknell of the Police Superintendents'
Association, 28.9.1980

Someone must be trusted. Let it be the judges.

Lord Denning, 23.11.1980

If you mention community relations to the ordinary policeman, he either falls about laughing or starts cursing.

Rev Robert Nind, Vicar of Brixton, 19.4.1981

It feels like being in hospital without the fear of pain or being in the army without fear of war.

Lord Kagan on prison life, 28.6.1981

Forget about the cosy image of Dixon of Dock Green.

Jim Jardine, Police Federation, 19.7.1981

A manifesto is issued to get votes and is not to be taken as gospel.

Lord Denning, 15.11.1981

In my view, the prisoners are extremely tolerant.

John Richardson, Governor of Leicester Prison, 6.12.1981

I am not saying that a girl hitching home at night should not be protected by law, but she was guilty of a good deal of contributory negligence.

Judge Bertrand Richards, in a rape case, 10.1.1982

29

I imagined that I would have kept about 21 of my friends from Parliament, but I've only kept one.

John Stonehouse, 24.1.1982

I don't think the British public would accept, and neither would I, the concept of the statutory black man.

Lord Scarman, 31.1.1982

Lawyers are honourable men and not a confederacy of smart Alecs.

Lord Edmund-Davies, 11.7.1982

I don't think anyone would dispute that lots and lots of people are denied justice.

Sir David Napley, 31.10.1982

Liberals, Social Democrats

If there is any emergence of a fourth party in British politics, it is the task of the Liberal Party to strangle it at birth.

Cyril Smith, 18.1.1981

The danger for any new party, at a time of disillusion with the old parties, is that it becomes all things to all men.

Shirley Williams, 29.3.1981

The only thing that isn't in it is being kind to animals.

Denis Healey, on the Social Democratic programme,
29.3.1981

I've always thought a stuff-'em-all party would poll a lot of votes.

David Penhaligon, MP (Lib), 25.10.81

If the old mould is being broken it looks like being replaced by a very familiar model, produced in a traditional political kiln belonging to Backbite and Bollocks.

Cyril Smith, 10.1.1982

If the qualities of this constituency did not seize my imagination, I would not seek to represent Hillhead.

Roy Jenkins, 21.3.1982

Love and Sex

It is wrong to label youngsters who may have a very loving relationship as criminals.

Dame Margaret Miles, 16.9.1979

I can't think why the term 'one-night stand' has such a pejorative tang.

Dudley Moore, 16.12.1979

I've always felt reading romantic novels was a bit like eating a whole box of chocolates or going to bed with a rotter. You can't stop because it's so nice, but afterwards you wish you hadn't.

Jilly Cooper, 17.2.1980

We love people at the wrong time for the wrong reasons.

Michael Korda, 27.4.1980

I have always been discriminating in my choice of lovers, but once in bed I am like a slave.

Britt Ekland, 13.7.1980

The more sex becomes a non-issue in people's lives, the happier they are.

Shirley MacLaine, 21.9.1980

Start loving yourself and you're finished.

Terry Wogan, 21.12.1980

Western romantic tradition has only ever accepted unsuitable love provided it ends in death — a tremendously wasteful concept.

Anna Raeburn, 10.5.1981

Hardy Amies once told me that the sexiest thing he had seen was nuns playing tennis.

Prudence Glynn, 5.7.1981

31

Some people lose control of their sluice gates of passion.

Workers' Daily, Peking, 2.8.1981

I was describing sexual intercourse without love, so you cannot call it love-making. What do you call it?

Susan Fleetwood, Royal Shakespeare Company, 17.1.1982

When a lady says no, she means perhaps. When she says perhaps she means yes. But when she says yes she is no lady.

Lord Denning, 17.10.1982

Marriage and Living Together

Everyone has the right to have two children.

Dr Patrick Steptoe, 9.9.1979

I do not believe mixed marriages are a sin before God.

Prime Minister Pieter Botha of South Africa, 30.9.1979

I believe marriage is the quickest way to ruin a relationship.

Shirley Bassey, 4.11.1979

People who wish to get married should meet before they decide to do so.

William Whitelaw, 18.11.1979

It's very dangerous if you keep love letters from someone who is not now your husband.

Diana Dors, 14.9.1980

There are many definitions of fidelity. Having a quick affair doesn't matter.

Trevor Howard, 4.1.1981

There are times and occasions when it would be marvellous to have a wife.

Cardinal Hume, 8.2.1981

When I'm married I want to be single, and when I'm single I want to be married.

Cary Grant, 3.5.1981

Boy friend is too juvenile. Lover is too limited. Live-in companion is awful. There is no accurate word.

Jessica Lange, 24.5.1981

A divorced wife with a house finds it easier to get remarried.

Lord Justice Ormrod, 24.5.1981

I married a doctor. I was going to marry the barmaid but she was on duty that night.

Richard Gordon, 21.6.1981

Weddings always end with people tearing each others' hair out.

Barbara Cartland, 12.7.1981

It is ridiculous to think you can spend your entire life with just one person. Three is about the right number. Yes, I imagine three husbands would do it.

Clare Booth Luce, 19.7.1981

No one asks a man how his marriage survives if he's away a lot.

Angela Rippon, 27.9.1981

I think the ideal relationship exists. But why is it so elusive?

Nell Dunn, 25.10.1981

Only one person in the world alters the vote of an MP — his wife.

Joe Ashton, MP, 15.11.1981

A good marriage is at least 80 per cent luck in finding the right person at the right time. The rest is trust.

Nanette Newman, 24.1.1982

Marriage is an act of will that signifies and involves a mutual gift, which unites the spouses and binds them to their eventual sons, with whom they make up a sole family — a domestic church.

Pope John Paul II, 31.1.1982

Although Great Passions may be possible without actually liking each other, marriages aren't.

Al Alvarez, 21.2.1982

I'll never get married again.

Elizabeth Taylor, 28.2.1982

I don't ask my husbands for anything. I give them presents when I leave them and never ask for alimony.

Zsa Zsa Gabor, on her sixth marriage, 18.4.1982

There is very likely to be some degree of infidelity in the course of a lifetime together.

Bishop of Winchester, 22.8.1982

Never marry a man who hates his mother because he'll end up hating you.

Jill Bennett, 12.9.1982

Marxism

Can you imagine lying in bed on a Sunday morning with the love of your life, a cup of tea and a bacon sandwich, and all you had to read was the *Socialist Worker?*

Derek Jameson, Editor, Daily Express, 11.11.1979

The Marxist analysis has got nothing to do with what happened in Stalin's Russia; it's like blaming Jesus Christ for the Inquisition in Spain.

Tony Benn, 27.4.1980

If the devil can quote scripture, surely a bishop can quote Lenin.

Bishop of Chester, 22.6.1980

In today's terminology Karl Marx could be labelled a 'monetarist'.

Milton Friedman, 26.10.1980

The Americans are the original Marxists. We invented the whole thing.

Arthur Miller, 16.11.1980

34

One good point about Marxism is that it recalled Christianity to its responsibilities.

Bishop Desmond Tutu, 26.4.1981

Brothers, I'm on my way before the remains of Karl Marx are disinterred from Highgate cemetery and reburied in Parliament Square.

Lord Cudlipp, 22.11.1981

A reconciliation of Marxism and political democracy is possible, urgent and necessary.

Tony Benn, 21.3.1982

Men

I have a big flaw in that I am attracted to thin, tall, good-looking men who have one common denominator. They must be lurking bastards.

Edna O'Brien, 1.7.1979

Although old Jonathan Cape was a bottom-pincher, he was also a bit of a prude.

Naomi Mitchison, 8.7.1979

I say I don't sleep with married men, but what I mean is that I don't sleep with happily married men.

Britt Ekland, 16.9.1979

It is men who face the biggest problems in the future, adjusting to their new and complicated role.

Anna Ford, 4.1.1981

The traditional figures of revolution, Rousseau, Karl Marx, Lenin and others, were no great emancipators of women and were themselves chauvinist. They left their wives slaving over a hot stove.

Sally Oppenheim, MP, 14.6.1981

However much men say sex is not on their minds all the time, it is most of the time.

Jackie Collins, 19.7.1981

Music and Musicians

Artists who say they practise eight hours a day are liars or asses.

Andres Segovia, 23.3.1980

I still have to fight this idea that I'm just a drummer.

Ringo Starr, 25.5.1980

The farther north you go, the better dancing you see.

Joe Loss, 25.5.1980

The festival is elitist, and I'm perfectly happy that it should be.

George Christie, Chairman of Glyndebourne, 1.6.1980

Bartok was a nice man.

Benny Goodman, 29.6.1980

Going back to the Beatles would be like going back to school.

John Lennon, 28.9.1980

I first became an adultress to the sound of Mozart.

Jacquetta Hawkes, 5.10.1980

I'm just as romantic as the next guy, and always was.

John Lennon, the day before his assassination, 14.12.1980

We are quite sure that Gilbert and Sullivan will survive.

Arts Council, on cutting off the D'Oyly Carte grant, 4.1.1981

What can I tell you? That the old man's mellowing?

Keith Richard on Mick Jagger, 20.9.1981

You know, sometimes I don't even like music.

Sir William Walton, 28.3.1982

An artist has to fight all his life against vanity.

Claudio Arrau, 21.11.1982

Newspapers and Journalists

It's not expensive to set up a newspaper.

Sir James Goldsmith, 16.9.1979

Journalism is a sure way of using up your intellectual capital.

John Maddox, Editor, Nature, 22.6.1980

The reality is that any journalist worthy of his salt would never reveal his sources because no one would ever talk to him again.

Greville Janner, MP, 3.8.1980

The *Sunday Times* will certainly be saved, although it might not be the same product.

Harold Evans, Editor, Sunday Times, 26.10.1980

Many of our institutions are under threat. *The Times* fights for them, and now *The Times* is going to fight for herself.

William Rees-Mogg, Editor, The Times, 26.10.1980

People seem to think they are doing me a favour in allowing me to take on something that is losing £13 million a year.

Rupert Murdoch, on his purchase of Times Newspapers, 15.2.1981

Great newspapers should not change hands as though they were packets of tea.

Lord Goodman, 22.3.1981

I never bugged anybody.

Chapman Pincher, 29.3.1981

You cannot inhibit a good journalist.

R W 'Tiny' Rowland, 29.3.1981

There seems to be a never-ending supply of corporate sugar-daddies attracted to the idea of owning a newspaper.

Lord Birdwood, 3.5.1981

A good journalist has a lot of shoe leather, a conscience and the ability to see the world from the wolf's point of view.

Fred W Friendly, 26.7.1981

Nobody west of Exeter ever reads the *New Statesman*.

Arthur Marshall, 27.9.1981

I am sick to death of Fleet Street. At times they act like lemmings.

Bill Keys, Chairman, TUC Print Committee, 4.10.1981

I am proud to be a muckraker when the cause is good.

Geoffrey Pinnington, Editor, Sunday People, *on its centenary*, 18.10.1981

I happen to believe that pregnancy is one of the most beautiful things you can see.

Lloyd Turner, Editor, Daily Star, *which had published photographs of the pregnant Princess Diana in a bikini*, 21.2.1982

In the world I live in nobody ever feels that their view has been fairly presented.

Tony Benn, 4.7.1982

India is the only developing country with a free Press.

Kuskwant Singh, Editor, Hindustan Times, 25.7.1982

A newspaper expresses its own view which is an amalgam of the view of its proprietor, its editor and the tradition it represents.

Daily Express, 15.8.1982

We have never had a free Press in this country.

Michael Meacher, MP, 3.10.1982

The Labour Party is paranoid about the media. The simple reason we get such a bad Press is that we do such damned silly things.

Conference delegate from Woking, 3.10.1982

Odd Information

We are used to people commenting about our address.

Valerie Winterton, who lives at 10 Downing Street, Halesowen, 30.12.1979

You're not at a party two minutes before someone sidles up with a letter that's been lost in the post for a fortnight.

Sir William Barlow, Post Office Chairman, 16.3.1980

It is extraordinary, but there are more horses in this country today than there were in the 1850s.

Angela Rippon, 31.8.1980

At the South Pole you find mostly Americans and emperor penguins.

David Attenborough, 24.1.1982

The things people do in the lifts of multi-storey car parks are beyond understanding.

Peter Davis, Sainsbury's, 7.2.1982

Mount Everest is now littered with junk from top to bottom.

Sir Edmund Hillary, 4.7.1982

I don't smoke, so neither does my office staff.

Sir Yue-Kong Pao, Hong Kong shipping millionaire, 15.8.1982

My mother was always the boss in the house.

Edda Mussolini Ciano, 21.11.1982

Parliament

There is a much more cheery atmosphere in the Commons than in the Lords.

Lord Butler of Saffron Walden, 13.4.1980

One day they are clients — the next day they are legislators passing these laws.

Spokesman for the English Prostitutes Collective, 27.4.1980

The House of Lords is a model of how to care for the elderly.

Frank Field, MP, 24.5.1981

There is a need for a second chamber whether it's called the Lords or not.

Joe Gormley, 2.8.1981

The British constitution reserves all its ultimate safeguards for a non-elected elite.

Tony Benn, 13.9.1981

The House of Commons is terribly outdated, an old man's club with too much spare-time boozing.

Shirley Williams, 6.12.1981

The only safe pleasure for a parliamentarian is a bag of boiled sweets.

Julian Critchley, MP, 13.6.1982

In my time there have been four Tory and two Labour masters of foxhounds in Parliament.

Jo Grimond, 15.8.1982

There is now no Labour MP south of a line from London to Bristol and no Conservative MP in the 13 divisions of the City of Glasgow.

Roy Jenkins, 17.10.1982

Inaccuracy is a way of life in this place.

Speaker George Thomas, 28.11.1982

Patriotism

I think it is probably still true that nationalism is stronger than any class feeling.

Fenner Brockway, 26.7.1981

I'm as anxious as anyone that the ship should be built in this country, but not at my expense.

Lord Matthews, Chairman of Cunard, 1.8.1982

Predictions

I am not interested in a third party. I do not believe it has any future.

Shirley Williams, 25.5.1980

I foresee a Liberal vote so massive and the number of Liberal MPs so great that we shall hold the initiative in the new Parliament.

David Steel, 14.9.1980

It is quite clear to me that the Tory Party will get rid of Mrs Thatcher in about three years time.

Sir Harold Wilson, 23.11.1980

Garlic, EEC directives, litres, *Lederhosen* are all part of the same thing and it is all going to lead, I imagine, to the giving away of Gibraltar.

Matthew Parris, MP (Con), 8.2.1981

South Africa will have a black Prime Minister within 10 years.

Bishop Desmond Tutu, 29.3.1981

Royalty

What I really need is a good wife.

Prince Charles, 3.6.1979

I can't think of a more wonderful thanksgiving for the life I have had than that everyone should be jolly at my funeral.

Earl Mountbatten, 2.9.1979

The succession is assured. There is no need for him to marry at all.

John Grigg on Prince Charles, 14.10.1979

There is a widely-held view, even among pro-monarchists, that nobody does more damage to the institution of royalty than this wayward woman.

William Hamilton, MP, on Princess Margaret, 6.4.1980

The thing I might do best is be a long-distance lorry driver.

Princess Anne, 24.8.1980

Actually sitting down and thinking is a sweat.

Prince Charles, 16.11.1980

Everything happens to the Royal Family in November.

Lady Diana Spencer, 30.11.1980

When he's not being Prince Charming, but working himself into a flap, you do notice that, if he were Mr Smith, he'd have bat ears and close-set eyes that can be nasty.

Daily Express *columnist on Prince Charles,* 25.1.1981

I don't think the Queen does interviews with people, and I can quite understand why.

Sir Robin Day, 15.2.1981

Everything always comes back to the same problem. There are too many people.

Prince Philip, 22.3.1981

There's a limit to how interesting a 40 acre field can be.

Princess Anne, 19.4.1981

I thank God I am British.

Prince Charles, 28.6.1981

Lady Diana Spencer is a direct descendant of Genghis Khan.

Professor Juan Balonso, Madrid genealogist, 26.7.1981

The bride is on the right.

Tom Fleming, BBC TV, on Lady Diana Spencer leaving with her father for her wedding, 2.8.1981

The whole thing is exactly like a Barbara Cartland story.

Barbara Cartland on the royal wedding, 2.8.1981

Our protection depends, I believe, on the mystical power which from time immemorial has been called God.

Prince Charles, 14.2.1982

Perhaps we should consider ourselves fortunate that Prince Charles did not deliver the baby himself.

The Spectator, 27.6.1982

Waste of bloody time. I'm sorry I came.

William Hamilton, MP, on his tea with the Queen,
4.7.1982

Bloody hell, Ma'am, what's he doing in here?

Elizabeth Andrews, chambermaid, on the intruder in
the Queen's bedroom, 18.7.1982

To ask the Queen for a cigarette is rock bottom.

Jeffrey Bernard, 18.7.1982

All the time I feel I must justify my existence.

Prince Charles, 5.9.1982

Prince Andrew is a 22-year-old man and I think that speaks for itself.

Buckingham Palace spokesman, on Prince Andrew's
holiday with Koo Stark, 10.10.1982

Seldom is there a quiet moment in the clan of Windsor, whose comings and goings never cease to delight the subjects of their tiny, sceptered isle.

Time, 17.10.1982

You must be joking. I'm not on a production line.

Diana, Princess of Wales, asked if she was pregnant again,
28.11.1982

Science and Discovery

The moon — like the South Pole — was reached half a century ahead of time.

Arthur C. Clarke, 15.7.1979

Space isn't remote at all. It's only an hour's drive away if your car could go straight upwards.

Sir Fred Hoyle, 9.9.1979

Most experiments don't work.

Frederick Sanger, Nobel prizewinner for chemistry, 19.10.1980

It is a remarkable fact that, genetically speaking, we are closer to the chimpanzee than, say, a horse is to a zebra.

Richard Leakey, 10.5.1981

Scientists should be on tap, not on top.

Sir Kelvin Spencer, former chief scientist, Ministry of Power, 7.2.1982

One of the surprises has been that the fish talk all day long.

Jacques-Yves Cousteau, on his survey of the Amazon, 17.10.1982

Schools and Universities

There is no right of 18-year-olds to read whatever subject they want at whatever cost with a guarantee of a job at the end.

Rhodes Boyson, 26.8.1979

Teachers ought to be curious about the qualities that have kept such comics as the *Dandy* and the *Beano* as children's favourites from one generation to another.

Brenda Thompson, Haringey Headmistress, 9.9.1979

It is difficult to believe that in a country that owns two million yachts we cannot afford to educate our children properly.

Baroness Phillips, 28.10.1979

Shrewsbury School in the mid-forties was as Stalinist as the Soviet Union.

Julian Critchley, MP, 23.12.1979

The days are long since passed when it was an advantage to have been educated at Eton.

Eric Anderson, headmaster-designate of Eton, 27.1.1980

One thing is certain: the rioters of Bristol did not suffer a surfeit of education and training opportunities.

Fred Jarvis, National Union of Teachers, 13.4.1980

Places like Eton and Harrow can be used for residential courses for trade unionists.

Labour Party Conference speaker, 5.10.80

We have a very serious problem on our hands, with many graduates leaving university without knowing the difference between an adverb and a preposition.

Colin MacCabe, Cambridge English Faculty, 25.1.1981

Academic staff rather enjoy coming to conclusions, but they don't like coming to decisions at all.

Lord Annan, 8.2.1981

Caretakers and dinner ladies are allowed to admit being homosexuals but teachers are not.

NUT conference speaker, 26.4.1981

The first class at Oxford, where I have examined, is an over-rated mark.

Lord Dacre (Hugh Trevor-Roper), 28.6.1981

I don't see it as the duty of government for every child up to the age of five to be looked after by the government.

Sir Keith Joseph, 1.11.1981

It has always been far too expensive to improve the education of working class children significantly.

Sir Angus Maude, 14.2.1982

My advice to members is to carry on caning.

*David Hart, National Association of Head Teachers,
28.2.1982*

Oxford and Cambridge are a major cancer in the educational system.

Labour Party discussion paper, 29.8.1982

The great majority of the products of today's independent schools are positively eager to combat the iniquities of the class system.

Michael St John Parker, Headmaster, Abingdon School,
19.9.1982

South Africa

I am a peace-loving person, but I am not a pacifist — there are some things worth dying for and human freedom could claim to be very high on the list.

Bishop Desmond Tutu, 1.6.1980

I don't need an agitator to tell me that I am forced to live in a ghetto, even if I do have a rather nice house in that ghetto.

Bishop Desmond Tutu, 6.7.1980

I don't believe my nation depends on these for survival.

*Prime Minister Pieter Botha, on the Mixed Marriages
and Immorality Acts*, 7.9.1980

Unless and until the dismantlement of apartheid is assured, it would be a grave mistake for South Africa to base her strategy on the assumption that when the chips are down the West will stand by her.

Edward Heath, in Johannesburg, 6.9.1981

There are some people who think that only folk with black faces have got feelings.

Prime Minister Robert Muldoon of New Zealand,
4.10.1981

The reason why most of humanity is sensitive about apartheid is because most of humanity is black.

Donald Woods, 7.3.1982

Soviet Union, Eastern Europe and Poland

We do not covet the lands or wealth of others.

Leonid Brezhnev, 20.1.1980

Communism stops only when it encounters a wall.

Alexander Solzhenitsyn, 17.2.1980

The attitude of all honest Afghans to Soviet troops is that of sincere hospitality and profound gratitude.

Tass, 16.3.1980

We do not accept that there are any prisoners of conscience in the Soviet Union.

Embassy spokesman in London, 4.5.1980

The Russians are not madmen.

Lord Home, 25.5.1980

There is far more religious faith in Russia than in England.

Graham Greene, 8.6.1980

One can divide only what one has generated by work.

Edward Gierek, 24.8.1980

We are demanding, not pleading.

Lech Walesa, 31.8.1980

The Soviet Union is not yet ready to take on that confrontation which could lead to World War III.

President Reagan, 8.2.1981

He who gives food to the people will win.

Lech Walesa, 23.8.1981

Our achievements leave class enemies breathless.

Leonid Brezhnev, 12.4.1981

In Poland everyone is a leader.

Lech Walesa, 7.6.1981

The Soviet State is not a very intelligent creature, rather a huge, brainless, antediluvian reptile with a fixed set of responses at its disposal.

Vladimir Bukovsky, 6.12.1981

The Soviet Union would remain a one-party nation even if an opposition party were permitted — because everyone would join that party.

President Reagan, 13.6.1982

Peace can only be upheld if we rely on the invincible might of the Soviet armed forces.

Yuri Andropov, 14.11.1982

Solidarity still exists inside us, even in those who deny it.

Lech Walesa, in a speech he was prevented from delivering, 19.12.1982

Sport

The only way the Government can prevent us taking part is by taking away the passports of all our competitors.

Sir Dennis Follows, British Olympic Committee, 6.1.1980

I'll cut his legs off and put him in a circus if he lets me down.

Mrs George Best on her husband, 24.2.1980

Anyone who can't score from a penalty needs shooting.

Graham Rix, 18.5.1980

The Soviet people don't like the Olympics because all the food is going to foreign visitors.

Ilya Dzhirkvelov, KGB defector, 25.5.1980

I have arranged for special music to be played all over Moscow to arouse positive emotions of courageous sport.

V J Kucharsky, Olympic Cultural Committee, 20.7.1980

Getting sacked is just part of the football scene.

Malcolm Allison, 12.10.1980

Everyone knows which comes first when it's a question of cricket or sex — all discerning people recognise that.

Harold Pinter, 12.10.1980

I took up boxing because it was the only way I could see of escaping from poverty.

John Conteh, 8.3.1981

Tennis is such an ego sport. It creeps into everything you do.

Sue Barker, 1.11.1981

I've never been fined for saying something obscene. It's always been for saying 'You're the pits' or something.

John McEnroe, 22.11.1981

I did not put a rose down my flies. I did not call Raman Subba Row [manager of the England cricket party in India] a wog. I did not ask for Ken Barrington's first-class ticket when he died.

Geoffrey Boycott, 28.2.1982

Don't tell me that unruly players don't incite crowd trouble because I've seen it happen.

Bobby Robson, 29.8.1982

We will never again in this country see a club pay £1 million for a player.

Peter Hill-Wood, Chairman of Arsenal, 19.9.1982

Sweeping Statements

Nothing can really change until the class system does.

Shirley Williams, 12.4.1981

If the United Nations would leave New York, nobody would ever hear of it again.

Mayor Ed Koch of New York, 21.2.1982

Show me a good loser and I'll show you a loser.

Paul Newman, 21.11.1982

Television and Radio

Let's face it, there are no plain women on television.

Anna Ford, 23.9.1979

Television — all it has ever done is to teach people how to tolerate mediocre entertainment.

Wilfrid Hyde-White, 30.9.1979

It seems only the other day that it was assumed that women were too emotional to broadcast news bulletins.

Baroness Wootton, 6.4.1980

When they ring you up at the BBC and ask you out to lunch, then you know you've been fired.

Jack de Manio, 1.2.1981

The most effective television I have ever seen, and have occasionally helped to make has always contained a ring of truth.

Desmond Wilcox, 31.5.1981

Bad language causes more upset among viewers than violence.

Leslie Halliwell, ITV, 13.9.1981

I can still do the Charleston. Who the hell can lead a coup against me?

Lord Grade, 13.9.1981

When all is said and done, a television set is a luxury.

Judge Watkin Powell, 6.12.1981

In my experience the people who get to the top of the heap and stay there are nice people.

Roy Plomley, 'Desert Island Discs', 31.1.1982

The fault of the BBC is not treachery but smugness.

Jo Grimond, 23.5.1982

You see the headlines saying kids are illiterate. They're not illiterate, they're just processing information in a different way.

American cable TV executive, 10.10.1982

Thatcher

We are not electing a President, we are choosing a Government.

Margaret Thatcher, 8.4.1979

One's advisers are not always right — and I often tell them so.

Margaret Thatcher, 29.7.1979

Mrs Thatcher is the most charismatic of the free world leaders.

Richard M. Nixon, 2.12.1979

Mrs Thatcher is doing for monetarism what the Boston Strangler did for door-to-door salesmen.

Denis Healey, 16.12.1979

No one would remember the Good Samaritan if he'd only had good intentions. He had money as well.

Margaret Thatcher, 13.1.1980

With regard to opinion in the Thatcher household, the Prime Minister does not have a monopoly.

Margaret Thatcher, 20.1.1980

I don't mind how much my Ministers talk, as long as they do what I say.

Margaret Thatcher, 27.1.1980

To stay in No 10 most prime ministers would eat their own grandmothers.

New Society, 10.2.1980

We don't sack a chap for one mistake.

Margaret Thatcher on James Prior, 2.3.1980

Margaret Thatcher doesn't smoke, but if she did you would hear the clash of gold-plated Ronsons every time she put a fag in her mouth.

Conservative MP quoted in The Guardian, 20.4.1980

I haven't the figure for jeans.

Margaret Thatcher, 4.5.1980

I like everything my beloved wife likes. If she wants to buy the top brick off St Paul's, then I would buy it.

Denis Thatcher, 14.9.1980

The badge 'Ditch the Bitch' is a disgrace to the Labour Party.

Schoolgirl at the Labour Party conference, 5.10.1980

You turn if you want. The lady's not for turning.

Margaret Thatcher, 12.10.1980

The Prime Minister should go and read her history books, starting from the Pilgrimage of Grace.

Michael Foot, 14.12.1980

I thought Margaret Thatcher was amazing.

Bob Hope, 1.3.1981

If this had not been in a church, I would have replied. I would have gone into them, wham, wham, wham.

Margaret Thatcher, on Left-wing heckling, 8.3.1981

The stated dose has not been exceeded.

Margaret Thatcher, 23.3.1981

To accuse me of being too inflexible is poppycock.

Margaret Thatcher, 1.11.1981

I'll stay until I'm tired of it. So long as Britain needs me, I shall never be tired of it.

Margaret Thatcher, 21.2.1982

We will resist the calls for easy options. Ulysses, you will remember, resisted the siren voices and came safely home to harbour.

Margaret Thatcher, 28.2.1982

I am extraordinarily patient, provided I get my own way in the end.

Margaret Thatcher, 4.4.1982

I used to be in favour of women priestesses but two years in the Cabinet cured me of them.

Norman St John-Stevas, 16.5.1982

I really would rather have been down there doing something practical. But someone had to be in No 10.

Margaret Thatcher, on the Falklands, 20.6.1982

I've been feeling inadequate for the last 29 years.

Carol Thatcher, 17.10.1982

Threats

If this disaster should ever materialise, I can assure Sir Derek Ezra that there will be a new ghost at Belvoir to haunt the Philistines of the Coal Board for ever.

Duke of Rutland, on plans to mine coal in the Vale of Belvoir, 30.3.1980

Whoever tries to climb over our fence, we shall climb over his roof.

President Saddam Hussein of Iraq, 27.7.1980

Trade Unions

If we want a society that is politically open, we have to understand that strikes are part of it.

Antonio Delfim Netto, Brazilian Planning Minister, 11.11.1979

I would never be party to attempts to smash up a democratically elected government.

Len Murray, 23.8.1980

You don't need opinion polls to tell you that trade union leaders do not represent their members' political views.

Frank Chapple, 21.9.1980

I've never bashed a union in my life.

Norman Tebbit, 18.10.1981

The most important lesson of all is to learn to listen to all your members, not just those who turn up for branch meetings.

Joe Gormley, 24.1.1982

When I make an agreement, the obligation of the membership is to honour it.

Sid Weighell, 24.1.1982

The money spent on strikes was one of the best investments we have made.

Sir Peter Parker, 25.7.1982

True

Concorde doesn't even have a movie.

Sir Freddie Laker, 24.8.1980

It is somewhat unfortunate that there is a problem in Ireland.

Mayor Ed Koch of New York, 21.6.1981

The navy isn't all wind and spray and yo-heave-ho.

Admiral Sir John Treacher, on his appointment as chairman of the Playboy Club, 12.7.1981

The meeting was not bad-tempered. It was not long enough to be tempered at all.

Coal Board Chairman Norman Siddall, on his three-and-a-half minute meeting with Arthur Scargill, 17.6.1982

Unemployment

It is difficult to strike if there's no work to go to in the first place.

Lord George-Brown, 24.2.1980

Unemployment is of vital importance, particularly to the unemployed.

Edward Heath, 30.11.1980

A substantial number of people of working age appear to have withdrawn, temporarily or permanently, from the labour force.

Bank of England Quarterly Bulletin, 21.12.1980

If there are many applicants for a few jobs, the job is overpaid.

Milton Friedman, 5.4.1981

Overmanning has been replaced by unemployment, a change which is miserable in human terms in the short run but eventually carrying a potential for national advantage.

John Biffen, 16.8.1981

Winston Churchill would turn in his grave at the thought of Mr Norman Tebbit being sent to the Department of Employment.

Michael Foot, 20.9.1981

The sooner dirty and dangerous jobs in industry are carried out by robots, the happier we will all be.

Norman Tebbit, 20.9.1981

Men and women denied the right to work will turn to violence.

Michael Foot, 27.9.1981

USA

My father always said: 'If it's on the table, eat it.'

Senator Edward Kennedy, 23.9.1979

It bewilders Americans to be hated.

Lance Morrow, 13.1.1980

Watergate is more easily forgiven as criminal folly than Chappaquiddick can be forgiven as an act of personal cowardice.

Graham Greene, 23.3.1980

Of the four wars in my lifetime, none came about because the US was too strong.

Ronald Reagan, 29.6.1980

The presidential system just won't work any more. Anyone who gets in under it ought not to be allowed to serve.

Gore Vidal, 31.8.1980

Recession is when your neighbour loses his job; depression is when you lose yours.

Ronald Reagan, 26.10.1980

I asked my daughter Amy what she thought was the most important question of our times, and she said nuclear weapons.

President Carter, 2.11.1980

My basic rule is that I want people who don't want a job in government.

President-elect Reagan, 16.11.1980

There is nothing wrong with America that together we can't fix.

President Reagan, 22.2.1981

Honey, I forgot to duck.

President Reagan, 5.4.1981

No one says anything bad about a turtle.

Patricia Riexinger, Office of Endangered Species,
19.7.1981

War, Peace and Weapons

The two superpowers often behave like too heavily-armed men feeling their way around a room, each believing himself in mortal peril from the other, whom he assumes to have perfect vision.

Henry Kissinger, 30.9.1979

Detente is like the race in 'Alice in Wonderland' where everyone had to have a prize.

Lord Carrington, 9.3.1980

The world knows, and above all the Soviets know, that no American President will sacrifice New York or Washington to save Berlin.

Richard M Nixon, 13.4.1980

Detente will not work unless there is deterrence.

Senator Edmund Muskie, 18.5.1980

The important thing when you are going to do something brave is to have someone on hand to witness it.

Michael Howard, MC, Chichele Professor of the History of War, Oxford, 18.5.1980

To adopt the nuclear disarmament option would be akin to behaving like a virgin in a brothel.

David Penhaligan, MP (Lib), 14.9.1980

There is no such thing as nuclear superiority once one has passed the level of deterrence.

Lord Zuckerman, 19.10.1980

There are contingency plans in the NATO doctrine to fire a nuclear weapon for demonstration purposes, to demonstrate to the other side that they are exceeding the limits of toleration in their conventional attack.

Secretary of State Alexander Haig, 8.11.1981

If nuclear war breaks out, whether in Europe or in any other place, it would inevitably and unavoidably assume a world-wide character.

Leonid Brezhnev, 8.11.1981

No NATO weapons, conventional or nuclear, will ever be used in Europe, except in response to attack.

President Reagan, 22.11.1981

I think it's 60 per cent likely that Western civilisation will destroy itself in 20 or 30 years' time.

E P Thompson, 20.12.1981

Even an inaccurate missile is quite a deterrent.

US Defence Secretary Caspar Weinberger, 18.4.1982

Let no one expect unilateral disarmament from us.

Yuri Andropov, 28.11.1982

Women

If women are treated as second-class citizens, they will behave like them.

Shirley Summerskill, MP, 20.1.1980

If women had been consulted more often, we should not be in half such a mess as we are today.

Baroness Llewelyn-Davies, 20.7.1980

Hair, in fact, is probably the bane of most women's lives

Joan Collins, 21.9.1980

We must recognise that now ladies are part of everyday life.

Secretary of the St Stephen's Club, 12.10.1980

Eighty-three per cent of the money is spent by women. They understand they can't spend more than the old man brings home.

Senator Barry Goldwater, 14.12.1980

This uncertain, floating me, whose existence I myself dispute, here it is, surrounded by an invisible troupe of women who perhaps should have received this honour long before, so that I am tempted to stand aside to let their shadows pass.

Marguerite Yourcenar, in her accession speech as the first woman member of the Academie Française, 25.1.1981

You can run the office without a boss, but you can't run it without secretaries.

Jane Fonda, 1.2.1981

We worked too hard and too long to get women and kids out of the pits to put them back there now; and I bloody well won't have a woman down a mine so long as I'm president.

Joe Gormley, 15.3.1981

A woman is like a teabag — only in hot water do you realise how strong she is.

Nancy Reagan, 29.3.1981

Too many people, especially women, are too well fed.

Reginald Bosanquet, 3.5.1981

It is a sad feature of modern life that only women for the most part have time to write novels, and they seldom have much to write about.

Auberon Waugh, 21.6.1981

I'm not saying women umpires are not so good. It's just harder to get upset with a woman in the chair.

John McEnroe, 21.6.1981

Motherhood is the most emotional experience of one's life. One joins a kind of women's mafia.

Janet Suzman, 19.7.1981

There is only one political career for which women are perfectly suitable: diplomacy.

Clare Booth Luce, 18.4.1982

Some of us have become the men we wanted to marry.

Gloria Steinem, founding editor of Ms magazine, New York, 4.7.1982

Women are getting stronger. But we're still in a transitional state, rather like trades unions.

Elizabeth Jane Howard, 11.7.1982

The hatch opens and there, in a green, tight-fitting sportsuit, accentuating her figure, is Svetlana. Her hair is combed prettily.

Soviet broadcast on the first woman to enter the Salyut 7 space station, 29.8.1982

Writers

If you put two spies on a bus they're much more attractive to the general reader than if you put them in a jet aeroplane.

John le Carré, 16.9.1979

It's always dangerous to write a book.

Norman Mailer, 18.11.1979

Writers of fiction are liars.

Edna O'Brien, 25.10.1979

The paragraph is a great art form. I'm very interested in paragraphs and I write paragraphs very, very carefully.

Iris Murdoch, 21.9.1980

I write when I'm inspired, and I see to it that I'm inspired at nine o'clock every morning.

Peter DeVries, 28.9.1980

I hadn't the courage for suicide, but it became a habit with me to visit troubled places.

Graham Greene, 5.10.1980

I know how foolish critics can be, being one myself.

Anthony Burgess, 2.11.1980

Truth is always duller than fiction.

Piers Paul Read, 12.4.1981

I'm all in favour of making up words if the one you want doesn't exist.

Tom Sharpe, 10.5.1981

A writer doesn't write to help humanity, but to help himself.

Graham Greene, 23.8.1981

Dedicating a book is like making love in public.

Arthur Hailey, 12.9.1982

Youth and Age

Youth looks forward, middle-age merely looks startled and old age looks back.

Lord Mancroft, **9.12.1979**

I don't want to see my face any more.

Lady Diana Cooper, **20.7.1980**

One of the many pleasures of old age is giving things up.

Malcolm Muggeridge, **21.12.1980**

As long as you can still be disappointed, you are still young.

Sarah Churchill, **24.4.1981**

The greatest problem about old age is the fear that it may go on too long.

A J P Taylor, **1.11.1981**

Most kids are born confident and then as they grow older it's knocked out of them.

Kim Wilde, **29.8.1982**

Zimbabwe

As far as I am concerned, he can touch down at the airport and sing 'God Save the Queen' until he is blue in the face.

Ian Smith, on Lord Soames arriving to take up direct rule in Southern Rhodesia, **16.12.1979**

After years of struggle, the British have understood.

Joshua Nkomo, **20.1.1980**

My mother said I could go to political meetings, but only if I came home in one piece.

Mrs Sally Mugabe, **9.3.1980**

It is now time to beat our swords into ploughshares.

Robert Mugabe, **9.3.1980**

Index